Uncommon Faith

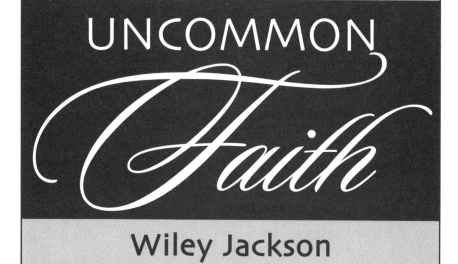

UNCOMMON Faith

Wiley Jackson

FOGHORN
PUBLISHERS
"Of Making Many Books There Is No End..."

Uncommon Faith

ISBN-10: 1-934466-24-7
ISBN-13: 978-1-934466-24-7

Printed in the United States of America
©2009 by Wiley Jackson. All Rights Reserved.

Foghorn Publishers
P.O. Box 8286
Manchester, CT 06040-0286
860-216-5622
foghornpublisher@aol.com
www.foghornpublisher.com

For information regarding speaking engagements, please send email to writewiley@wileyjackson.org , or written correspondence to Wiley Jackson, P.O. Box 339, Stone Mountain, Georgia 30086

Dedication

I would like to dedicate this book to my wife Mary; my sons, Wiley and Paul; to my mother Bobbie; my brothers and sisters: Pastor Rodney, Cynthia, Beverly and Jerrick.

To Apostle Price and Dr. Betty who taught me to be uncommon in my faith, and to the Price family.

To the Gospel Tabernacle family, who I owe the highest debt to, and to the other partners and friends who have supported me through the years; I constantly pray and know that God will continue to give you His very best.

Bishop Jackson

Partners

Special Thanks to My Platinum Elite Partners

It is because of dedicated partners that we are able to keep the ministry of publishing alive and available to people all over the world. Thank you for your seed, and may God richly add His grace to your life.

Pastor Mark Baker

Deaconess Lavonne Barber

Tim Gray

Deacon Eliot and Sondra Harrison

Elder John and Monica Pearson

Deacon Reginald and Deaconess Sharon Ponder

Elder Delbert and Deaconess Flor Warner

Dr. Renee Williams

Lafayette Brazil

Tracy and Ryan Stein

Pamela Fedrick

Demetrius and Deaconess Sharon Hammitt

Dr. Rhonda Ross

Nathaniel and Glynder Smith

Mr. and Mrs. Michael A. Wood

Table of Contents

1

Being Uncommon
in a Common World

One of the most difficult challenges that you will ever face in life is to maintain your identity in a world constantly seeking to change you into its image. There is nothing more satisfying and easy to most people than just being like every-body else. Really, just think about it. You don't have to do much of anything special to be common these days. All you have to do is simply fit in with the in-crowd. And by the way, the in-crowd has made it quite easy to get into. All you have to do is nothing special, nothing extraordinary, and nothing uncommon, and hey, you're in.

The requirements for entry are so minimal that anybody can get in. While that might sound like a good proposition to some, to God it doesn't sound all that good. From the beginning of time until now, God has been seeking out people who will stand out and be distinctive despite what the masses are doing and just be different. God is looking for somebody to be uncommon in a common society where most people are completely satisfied with just barely getting by. Now when I talk about barely getting by, I'm not just talking about money.

Most people can't seem to see things outside of the context of money. While money is a major issue in life, and that we cannot deny, there are still more things of greater significance than money. In life, common folks get by with the bare necessities of everything. They barely get an education. They barely raise their kids up to be responsible. They barely go to church. They barely get involved in the community. They barely speak out on valid issues. This list can go on forever. I think that you are getting my point. God never called you to barely get by. God called you to live an extraordinary life. And that's what this book is all about, Uncommon Faith that yields extraordinary results.

However, the only way that you can receive extraordinary results, is by choosing to be uncommon even though the majority of the world chooses the be ordinary. You have got to overcome the pressure of being like everybody else and just make the choice to do things God's way, even if it's not comfortable at first. Today the word Christian has become very common; so much so that very few people in secular society even respect the title Christian. When you think about it, you really can't blame them for their viewpoint. There isn't anything that really distinguishes Christians from anybody else in the world other than a whole list of negative stereotypes. There was a time when just being a Christian meant that you were uncommon.

"There was a time when just being a Christian meant that you were uncommon"

People of the world would look at the church and see a clear difference in the way we talked, how we dressed, the places that we went, and even what we listened to. We were clearly uncommon. But what happened? Because of our desire to fit in, and to be like everybody else, we began to compromise our standards and we finally gave in and became just like the ones we stood out from. At one time we were proud of our distinction. Now many believers are ashamed to be considered different, as if there is something wrong with being different.

Why should you be embarrassed because you are recognized for being different, especially if your difference is a Godly one? In reality, we had a much purer faith then, than we do now. I'm not saying that the church should not have moved forward and progressed on different issues. I thank God that we have moved away from meaningless traditions of men. Believe me when I tell you that I am not trying to put the church back into bondage and legalism. Thank God for freedom, and thank God we've moved on. I'm simply trying to convey to you the mindset of how the church used to view being uncommon.

While being uncommon today, particularly in the body of Christ, makes some people feel ashamed, back then being uncommon was worn like a badge of honor.

It didn't make a difference what people in the world, and of the world, had to say, the saints of old continued to embrace their identity as people of God. They would say, "I'm in the world but not of the world." They knew that they were put here on earth, not to fit in but to stand out.

I beseech you therefore, brethren, by the mercies of God, that ye present your bodies a living sacrifice, holy, acceptable unto God, which is your reasonable service. And be not conformed to this world:

but be ye transformed by the renewing of your mind, that ye may prove what is that good, and acceptable, and perfect, will of God.
—*Romans 12:1-2*

You're Not Supposed to Fit In

You are called to be different, different in every way. As strange as it may seem, you were meant to be uncommon. *Dictionary.com* defines the word uncommon as not common, unusual, rare: unusual in amount or degree. From this definition we can conclude that that which you have too little of, you should have more of, if you want to be uncommon. Getting C's in high school and college is pretty common, but the uncommon students want a greater degree of knowledge so they go beyond the basic expectations. They study harder when everybody else is partying, watching TV, and playing their Playstations.

"I don't know what the secret to success is, but I know that the secret to failure is in trying to please everybody."

I like the idea of uncommon as being above the ordinary, exceptional, and remarkable. You weren't put on this earth to live and die, and that's all. You weren't put on earth to fit in either. You were placed here to make a difference. And in making that difference you won't always be the most popular guy in town. In fact if you are popular with everybody, then something is wrong. Everybody may know the most popular people, but the most popular guy rarely stands for anything, because he is so busy trying to please everybody.

Back in the eighties, which now seem so long ago, actor and comedian Bill Cosby, who at the time was the richest African-American, was asked what the secret to success was. He paused a moment, and then responded, "I don't know what the secret to success is, but I know that the secret to failure is in trying to please everybody." Wow, that statement is really powerful, and definitely true. Trying to please everybody, which includes trying to fit in, is the first sign that you are on the road to a catastrophe. Just think about how much trouble comes from trying to fit in.

All over the world, especially in urban areas, kids join gangs trying to fit in. Although they know that they are risking their lives by being a part of a dangerous bunch of criminals, they still want to fit in. I understand that isn't the only reason, and that many of these young people are longing for family in any way they can find it, but the basis of their connection still lies in wanting to fit in, rather than stand out.

Corrupt politicians try their best to fit in by being the same as other corrupt politicians instead of leading the pack with integrity. Their mindset says, "Well everybody else is corrupt, so this is just the expected norm." Again, I repeat, you are not called to fit in. You are called to stand out! When you've been given a special assignment to do in life, you are marked by that call.

Everything about that calling identifies who you are. Based on that, all of your thoughts, your every move, and the way that you act and react are totally centered upon your assignment. I'm sure you've heard of Bill Gates. Well if you haven't he has been and still may be the richest man in the United States of America. At one time, for a very long time, he was actually the richest man in the world. Well Mr. Gates was not called to fit in. In fact, he never really fit in any group, other than that which dealt with computers and computer programming.

His life seemed to have been planned by God, so much so, that his early steps as a teenager were orchestrated in such a way that he was afforded opportunities to practice writing computer programs at a nearby college long before comput- ers were available in a personal computer (PC) format. He was actually a part of a computer club, probably one of the first in the nation, while in high school. Gates wasn't dreaming about making the NFL or the NBA. He wasn't trying to be cool like all the jocks. His one aim was simply to perfect the seed that started inside of him.

You see, success in life, and better yet success in God's eyes is not defined the way that society defines it. Success in God's eyes can be simplified down to one thing—doing whatever He told you to do. John the Baptist was called to preach one message. His entire career was reduced to just one simple, not so provocative message—REPENT. In fact, the message that he preached is still one that so many millions today need to understand, how to change their minds, and turn toward God, which is exactly what repentance is. Imagine if John the Baptist lived in our modern era, folks would have laughed him to scorn.

They would have ruthlessly made fun of him, laughing at his wilderness clothes. Preachers would actually be the worst critics of John the Baptist, because he wouldn't have had the most in style fashions, custom tailored Oxford suits, alligator shoes, and Brioni ties. He wouldn't have gotten any invitations to the main conferences to speak because they would have said he couldn't preach, since he only had but one message. He couldn't sing, he couldn't whoop, he had just one message.

But in God's eyes he was a major success. He didn't fit in; he didn't have to. All he had to do is one thing. Obey God! In the final analysis, that's really all that matters.

> *Brethren, I count not myself to have apprehended: but this **one thing I do**, forgetting those things which are behind, and reaching forth unto those things which are before, I press toward the mark for the prize of the high calling of God in Christ Jesus.*
> *—Philippians 3:13-14 (bold author's own)*

Uncommon Serving

Sometimes I feel like a reformer in that I am trying to get the body of Christ to recognize her original call. We've drifted so far away, but now it's time to come back to where we belong. The whole basis of true Christianity is all about serving, not about being served. Jesus even said that if you really want greatness in life, you have to learn how to serve.

> *And he said unto them, The kings of the Gentiles exercise lordship over them; and they that exercise authority upon them are called benefactors. But ye shall not be so: but he that is greatest among you, let him be as the younger; and he that is chief, as he that doth serve. For whether is greater, he that*

sitteth at meat, or he that serveth? is not he that sit-teth at meat? but I am among you as he that serveth. —Luke 22:25-27

Jesus, our perfect example shows us that being a servant is the highest calling. This is the original plan of God, to create servants in the kingdom of God who will unselfishly go out and win the lost. We are sons and daughters in the kingdom of God, but in the church of the Lord Jesus, we are servants, called by God to accomplish His mission in the earth. I've always loved the spirit of a true servant. True servants are uncommon. I respect all of our armed forces, those who have given their lives, and those who put their lives at risk to protect our freedom. I have an enormous amount of respect for these young men and women.

"Jesus, our perfect example shows us that being a servant is the highest calling."

However, and I don't want anyone to take this out of context, although I totally respect all servicemen, I tend to have a higher value for those who willingly signed up to serve our country. They went and served because they wanted to do so. Their heart was totally into the idea of sacrificial service, fully knowing that this kind of service could possibly cost them their lives. That's uncommon. It's this kind of heart that sets these servicemen apart from all the rest. Just to let you know, any person can choose to become an uncommon serviceperson at anytime. You don't necessarily have to have started with this in mind. Perhaps this book is helping you to come into a better understanding, and from now on, you will choose the uncommon way of service.

Those who sign up for the army are making a statement to their country and the world that they are willing to die in service to protect the freedom of the nation. Not many people are willing to surrender on this level. God is looking for some uncommon servants who will go into areas where service is needed and become a solution to ailing problems in society. There are so many problems in our world today. Often, we hear people complain about these problems, yet do absolutely nothing about it.

"You are called to fix any problem that really bothers you."

Personally, I get irritated when people always have something to talk about negatively yet do nothing at all to even try to fix it. You are called to fix any problem that really bothers you. That is how you can be of service to the world. There are many examples of people who saw a problem and decided to do something about it. Take Mother Teresa for example:

The daughter of an Albanian grocer, she went to Ireland in 1928 to join the Sisters of Loretto at the Institute of the Blessed Virgin Mary and sailed only six weeks later to India as a teacher. She taught for 17 years at the order's school in Calcutta [Kolkata].

In 1946 Sister Teresa experienced her "call within a call," which she considered divine inspiration to devote herself to caring for the sick and poor. She then moved into the slums she had observed while teaching. Municipal authorities, upon her petition, gave her the pilgrim hostel near the sacred temple of Kali where she founded her order in 1948. Sympathetic companions soon flocked to her aid. Dispensaries and outdoor schools were organized. Mother Teresa adopted Indian citizenship, and her Indian nuns all donned the sari as their habit. —(Encyclopedia Britannica 2005)

Wow, what an unbelievable life of extraordinary service. Committing to become a nun alone is an uncommon desire, yet Mother Teresa took it even further than that. She didn't just want to live her life as a common nun, a nun willing only to do what was average. Mother Teresa finished college and could have easily become a teacher at one of the many prestigious Catholic Universities or Catholic high schools around the world. Instead she chose the lesser-traveled path of the uncommon and gave her life wholeheartedly to the struggle of the poorest people perhaps in the world in Calcutta.

Hers is an example not only of service, but also of uncommon service. Mahatma Ghandi decided to serve his country of India by leading a non-violent movement, opposing the British rule. Dr. Martin Luther King Jr. followed his example years later, by giving his life to extraordinary service leading the civil rights movement in the United States. It's not only famous people who qualify as uncommon servants but also thousands of not so famous people who also serve in an above average way everyday.

Firefighters in general are uncommon servants, but even more so are those who bravely sought to save the lives of the victims trapped inside the aftermath of the World Trade Centers on 9/11. These are no ordinary servants at all. They are uncommon. Going far beyond the call of duty, they put everything on the line, to serve in such a way that may not always make them popular, but they will always be definitely heard, respected, and remembered.

What Do You Do When The Stakes Are Against You?

Okay you realize that you are supposed to be living the "uncommon life." Let me caution you; the uncommon road is not paved with roses. It's a road that can be a bit lonely at times, but the rewards are great. I know all too well that there are so many people who are against this message and will fight you so that you will never come into the fullness of what God intended you to be. We don't live in an "uncommon-friendly" world. As a pastor I know that there are many leaders who are not really concerned with teaching people how to become uncommon, but rather teach the masses how to play it safe in life. So what do you do when there isn't really a whole lot of support for your "uncommonness"?

"Let me caution you; the uncommon road is not paved with roses."

First, find someone already getting the results that you are seeking and align yourself with him or her. Next, start taking massive action, the same kind of action they've taken. The whole basis of our mission has always been to get people to take action. Just do something. The fact that you have read up to this point signifies that you are an action taker. The more action you choose to take within the context of that thing that you are called to do, in time will distinguish you from the rest. I'm not telling you that it's going to be easy. But it will be worth it. Most people really dislike change. And becoming an uncommon person will require change.

But without change we will never move forward. That's why we no longer ride horse and buggies, because someone wanted change. And you, my reader, are on point to changing your environment. You can do it! But you won't do this in an ordinary way, not in a common way, because common folks don't make changes. They just stay the same. Don't get too overwhelmed though. You are not obligated to change every individual, but you have to start somewhere. Start by making a difference with just one person, maybe even yourself. Then in time you'll eventually change the world!

2

Uncommon Faith

There are literally hundreds of millions of titles that have been released in this world ever since writing began. In fact, nearly every second of the day, someone somewhere is writing a new book. With all of these books in heavy circulation, what makes the Bible so spectacular and unique amidst a great number of competing books? With so many books to choose from, people continue to choose the Bible as the number one reference book in the world. To date, the Bible has sold more than seven billion copies worldwide and has been translated into nearly every language.

Ministries such as Wycliffe Bible translators are steadily translating this amazing work into languages of indigenous tribes, where no established system of language has ever been recorded in writing. The Bible is the all-time bestselling book ever. I believe the reason so many people embrace this work is because it offers the world much needed hope, and people always need hope. Our society is definitely in search of the answers that the Bible clearly addresses, but added to that, people need to have some consolation that things will get better, that eventually they'll make it.

Equally as important though is that the Bible offers its readers a basis and a how-to formula for living by faith. Like no other book in the world, the Bible chronicles and lists people that operated in extraordinary faith against unbelievable odds. These stories give people everywhere hope to know that if someone else has achieved freedom in a particular area, then they too can achieve the same success by following the same principles. Although there are many people in the Bible that appear to be extraordinary giants of faith, I believe more accurately that these people are just ordinary people with uncommon faith in an extraordinary God.

That's the one thing that distinguishes "faith people" from those not strong in faith. It's not so much that we are so big, but rather that God is so big. People with uncommon faith continue to believe in a great God to do the impossible, even when they witness destruction and devastation everyday of their lives. There are so many things that God did in my life, personally and throughout the course of my ministry, that I am amazed by. Looking back, I am convinced that there is no way that I could have done any of those things on my own. It was all God.

"Every spectacular thing that happened in my life was all a direct result of me believing in a God who could do anything."

Every spectacular thing that happened in my life was all a direct result of me believing in a God who could do anything. But where did I get the courage to operate in this kind of uncommon faith? Did I just wake up one day and start doing great things? The truth is, I began to see examples in the scriptures that caused me to see God in a totally different light. Through other people's examples, I began to develop faith for things that would otherwise be written off as impossible. How do you build a great church for God, buy prime property and launch a nationwide television ministry, not having the money to do so?

The only way that somebody could do this is by believing in a God who cannot fail. God and His word built me up to believe that I could do anything, so I believed. Uncommon faith tells me not to look at what I can see, but to rather look at what I cannot see and believe it is there. That's biblical faith. That is uncommon faith. It takes a certain kind of person, someone that seems to be out of their mind, to believe God can do extraordinary things. I've already told you in the first chapter that we live in an ordinary world where people expect you to do things in a common way.

Going beyond the expectation of everyday people automatically labels you as being an uncommon soul. Truth is, nothing of great magnitude ever gets accomplished in life unless common folks began to step out in uncommon faith and believe God for uncommon results. I'll have to admit that at first flowing in this uncommon arena can be frightening because you really don't know what's going to happen. You really don't have a point of reference at all. You have to hold onto your faith which at times doesn't seem too substantial. It's an abstract idea, something that you can't physically hold on to, but that is why you must understand that it is faith which gives you the substance to create the things you hope for. Faith is substance!

Now faith is the substance of things hoped for, the evidence of things not seen. —Hebrews 11:1

Abraham—The Father of Uncommon Faith

Abraham is known in the three largest religions, Christianity, Islam, and Judaism, as a man of great faith. He is arguably considered the father of all three religions as well. Why is it that Abraham is considered to be such a man of extraordinary faith? I've never seen anywhere in the scriptures Abraham in and of his own power doing anything really spectacular. In fact, when God told Abraham that he would give birth to a child while in his old age, he laughed hysterically, knowing that his reproductive organs had probably stopped working a long time ago. Besides, the probability of a man nearly 100 years old having his first child was close to impossible. Even in a society lacking the scientific knowledge that we have today, Abraham understood that this would take a miracle. He knew that he could never do something so extraordinary acting alone.

> *Then Abraham fell on his face and laughed, and said in his heart, "Shall a child be born to a man who is one hundred years old? And shall Sarah, who is ninety years old, bear a child?"*
> *—Genesis 17:17*

Think about it, Abraham, laughed at God. It's one thing to laugh at the words of people who have no ability to fulfill their commitment, but it's a totally different thing to laugh at God.

Not only did Abraham laugh, but his wife Sarah, who was eavesdropping on their conversation, began to laugh as well when she heard about God's ridiculous plans. You will know for sure that you are operating in uncommon faith when you begin pursuing a promise that seems totally ridiculous. Some people say they have faith and need it to make it from one day to the next. Some people say they have faith to simply pay their bills.

"You will know for sure that you are operating in uncommon faith when you begin pursuing a promise that seems totally ridiculous."

Others say they have faith to know where their next meal is coming from. Hey, everybody is different. What we need and use faith for depends entirely on our own situations and I'm not suggesting that those things don't require faith. But in a country as blessed as the United States of America, getting those things may require just a few simple changes. You may need to work more hours, find a better job or start a home-based business. Maybe you may need to find out which social organization, church or family member is willing to offer you food and help for your family.

"What we need and use faith for depends entirely on our own situations..."

Now I recognize that there are people in the United States who deal with hunger on a daily basis and for those people, it will require faith to eat. The point that I am making to the greater population is that it is not ridiculous to believe God will provide your next meal, unless of course you live in a country or region where no one eats on a regular basis. But where everybody is eating food on a daily basis, sometimes three, four, and five times a day, it's not all that uncommon to expect a dinner.

To believe that you will have your first child when you are at the age of becoming a great, great, great grandfather sounds pretty ridiculous, even for the most optimistic person. Although Abraham laughed at first, he quickly began to remember how awesome his God actually was. He began to ponder over the other times that he believed God by simply taking Him at His Word. God told Abraham to leave his country and his family and go to a place that He would show him. Not many people will just uproot their family and move to a place that they have never been to and know nothing about just because a faceless voice tells them to.

It takes a person of uncommon faith to obey God when you really don't have an idea of what God is actually talking about. You simply believe Him because He said it, and you trust that whatever God said, He would surely bring to fruition. Abraham became the Father of Uncommon Faith, because he chose to believe that God would do some of the most unusual things through his life. The promise of Isaac came to pass, just as God said it would. Even though the whole idea was absolutely absurd, believing that he and his wife could bare children in their nineties, he still trusted God's Word through faith.

Through this he became the father of faith. You too can become one of the fathers of faith by simply believing that God can do the impossible. The thing that you will bear in the spirit will be the gift of God that only faith can produce. Are you willing to allow God to use you to perform unusual miracles? Will you be willing to deal with the laughter and ridicule of the people, your family and your friends? If you are, then maybe you too are ready to walk in the realm of the uncommon and receive all of the rewards that go along with being uncommon.

"You, too, can become one of the fathers of faith by simply believing that God can do the impossible."

I can remember when I began my pastorship, I was a young man just in my twenties. We started off in a little storefront church that could barely seat eighty people. It was there that I made the choice to believe God for big things. I chose to believe in a big God who could provide big things for me. It was while we were in this small storefront church that God told me to go on television. It would have been a pretty common concept to go on television had we boasted a thousand or more members, because we would have had the financial backing to do so. That wasn't the case at all. Back then, all I had was faith in a great big God, but that was all.

I didn't have a budget, a big staff or any multimillionaire donors that could just write a ten million dollar check to get us on television and pay the bill for a year or so. All I had was one word from God—Go! I can imagine how Abraham must have felt when God told him to go, or for that matter, when Jesus told Peter to come as Peter boldly began to walk on water. They both received just one word, and on that word were expected to do something that they had never done before.

That is what uncommon faith is all about, doing what you have never done before. Uncommon faith is all about doing what you never thought you could do. It was totally beyond my comprehension how we should run a television ministry: how to buy time, how to market our ministry to masses and so on. None of those things were familiar territory to me. None of those things really mattered either. What did matter was my willingness to obey God, and not having much to begin with, embrace the reality that if God told me to do something that He is all-wise enough to provide me with every resource that I would need to get the job done.

When I began in ministry I didn't have a whole lot of people who were doing uncommon things. I mean, most people were winning souls to Christ and reaching the lost, but not in an uncommon way. Most of the preachers were pretty much doing the same thing everybody else was doing. There was something within me that wanted to do things totally differently, not just for the sake of being different, but for the sake of letting the world know how big my God really is. I felt that He had empowered me to show everyone that a change in faith was necessary in order for Him to fully provide and prove His love to us.

So in the beginning, I got all of my food and spiritual sustenance from the Word of God and the numerous stories in the Bible of people that God used in uncommon ways to do uncommon things. My thought both then and now was, if God could use them to do the impossible, then surely He could use me too. With that, I began my journey of doing what God said, and finding people of faith doing the same.

Surrounding Yourself with Uncommon People

There are a few things that have a direct correlation to your faith. One of those things is acting on God's Word, or as I like to say, the Word in Action. However, another important thing is the people that you surround yourself with. They have a major impact on the way that you perceive God; they can affect whether you will do great things and whether or not you will take the necessary action in life to yield amazing results. Really, your company and your inner circle have a great deal of influence on the way you think. That is why it is so crucial to keep watch over whom you allow in your life. Negative people will only bring negativity to your thinking and affect every aspect of your life, even if you are not aware of the direct result. Likewise, positive people will subconsciously motivate you to look at things in a more positive way, ultimately affecting how you operate.

Negative people will only bring negativity to your thinking and affect every aspect of your life, even if you are not aware of the direct result.

I love people! Sometimes that goes without saying. There are some people though, that may not understand why I choose not to allow them into my inner circle. It's not because I feel like I'm above them or that I look down on any person. My thing is that I realize I have a definite mission in life and I really don't have time for anyone who is trying to interrupt my progress, or even someone just unwilling to help me in my pursuit. Both of these groups will hinder my efforts and slow me down. So, I intentionally want to be around uncommon people, because it helps me to keep the "uncommon edge" I need in order to accomplish God's will in my life.

For many years now, I've surrounded myself with my mentor, Dr. Frederick K.C. Price, who has been rightly called the Apostle of Faith. There is one main reason that I associate with him: he displays extraordinary faith. He definitely knows what it means to walk in uncommon faith. Dr. Price built the Faith Dome at Crenshaw Christian Center in Los Angeles, California that was for many years the largest sanctuary in the United States of America. Today it is still the largest facility in America originally built as a sanctuary, containing 10,146 seats. Yet, Dr. Price did not grow up in a pastor's home.

He didn't have the legacy of preaching prowess being passed down from one generation to the next. Before he settled down in the Word of Faith movement, he had pastored in four different denominations; prior to that he was a paper cutter. Nothing about him or his previous character would have led me to believe that he would one day become the founding pastor of one of the nations' largest churches, beginning with only nine members and growing to more than 18,000 people. How did this Santa Monica native ride this wave and discover such success in ministry? He did it the same way that Abraham did it, the same way that Prophet Elijah did it and also how Jesus the Christ did it.

Dr. Price obeyed the voice of God regardless of how ridiculous God's Word sounded. When people talked about him, he kept on believing what God said; his ministry is a living testament to this. So as I began to develop in my faith, I knew that I wanted the kind of faith present in his life working in my life also. The best way for me to tap into that kind of flow was to get around him and people that are like him. Like always begets like. Broke people always keep company with other broke people. Rich people fellowship among each other. According to the scripture, even fools travel in packs.

> *The desire accomplished is sweet to the soul: but it is abomination to fools to depart from evil. He that walketh with wise men shall be wise: but a companion of fools shall be destroyed.*
> *—Proverbs 13:19-20*

The scripture calls the gang of fools a "companion of fools." It suggests that if you keep company with the wise you'll become wise but on the other hand, if you keep company with fools, you'll become a fool as well. You are the company that you keep. In fact, everything that you are experiencing in life, both good and bad, can in some way be contributed to your inner sphere of influence. If you want uncommon faith, hang out with people that possess uncommon faith. If you can't think of anyone, then hang out with me.

"You are the company that you keep."

I'm not saying that to brag, I just know who I am and what I am put on this earth to do. When you keep company with common people they will force you to become just like them. No one really likes it when your very existence makes him or her feel exposed. When you are an uncommon person, it often makes people begin to evaluate themselves, asking questions like, "Where am I lacking and how can I improve?" Don't give into the pressure of trying to accommodate the masses. Don't compromise. Whatever it is that you do in life, associate only with those that are even better at doing it than you are because, in time, their faith will rub off on you and you will begin to believe God for the impossible too.

3

Uncommon Pursuits

For nearly a decade or more, we have witnessed a culture that has been carried away by the winds of mediocrity. It is my heart's cry that the message in this book will once again bring us back to the place where pursuing greatness was once commonplace. As a child I always heard about people who did great things. Many of them have made a mark on society that will never be erased. Dr. Martin Luther King is one such person who has clearly made an uncommon contribution to society at large.

Although Rev. Dr. Martin Luther King Jr. is perhaps the most well known and surely the most remembered civil rights activist of all times, Dr. King was not alone in his lofty pursuit for freedom and justice for all people. There were many other luminaries of that time who helped to blaze the trail that Dr.

King once trod. Rev. Ralph Abernathy, Rev. Wyatt Walker, Rev. Fred Shuttlesworth and Rev. Joseph Lowery, the minister who was selected to give the closing prayer at President Barack Obama's inauguration, were just among a few of the many leaders of that era who chose to do things in the most uncommon way.

For them uncommon pursuits were typical. Dr. Vernon Johns, an incredible and respected preacher and civil rights activist, was actually Dr. King's mentor. He held the pastorate at the Dexter Avenue Baptist Church in Montgomery, Alabama, the church King later presided over. Dr. John's approach to civil justice was far more radical and controversial than most people before or after him as he took the uncommon and lonely road to make sure that the poor and disadvantaged people in society could have a voice during a time when people of color were simply not being heard.

If I tried to name all of the unspoken heroes during that time it would take hours. These uncommon people could be found in all areas of life, not only ministry and social activism. Even in the area of business, there were literally thousands of rags to riches stories that happened from the early 1900's until the 1980's here in America. Many of these stories of how immigrants came from Europe, the Caribbean, Africa, and parts of

South America and began start-up businesses with borrowed money or even no money at all, are quite amazing.

It's incredible to witness how common people pursued uncommon dreams and received extraordinary results in the process. Pursuing greatness used to be the expected norm; history proves this for us. Somehow modern society has fooled us into believing that there is something wrong with dreaming big and going for greatness in life. They have made you to feel that something is wrong, sinful, and even immoral about pursuing the best that life has to offer. The finest that life has to offer should be reserved for somebody, right? My thought is, "Why not me? Why not you?"

The sad thing is that many people in the church world have embraced this whole notion of living life in pursuit of nothing. Yeah, you read correctly, there are so many people who really don't have any concrete plans for their lives, no preparations for their future, no intention on doing anything of real value in this world. I call that living in pursuit of nothing. And trust me when I tell you that that isn't really hard to do. The problem with this is that when people pursue nothing in life, not only do they get nothing but they also find themselves living in hopeless situations.

The problem with this is that when people pursue nothing in life, not only do they get nothing but they also find themselves living in hopeless situations.

This is the common condition of mankind. And it's going to take an uncommon person with an uncommon mind to confront this problem head on. Even as I travel around the country I'm saddened when I see so many people, thousands, who have so much potential, so much promise, so much to offer in life, yet produce so little. Honestly, I don't even have to leave my own city to see how many people are living their lives at the lowest levels, pursuing nothing. When the few people begin to pursue something, it is usually something so common that it doesn't get anyone's attention, not even God's.

My whole point is that when you die you are going to be remembered for what you pursued when you were alive. If you pursued an uncommon dream people will always remember you. If not, your memory will fade like a vapor. What will you be remembered for when you are gone? More than that, what are you known for right now?

My whole purpose is to provoke you to really think about where you are now, and where you could actually be if you shed the opinions of others and began to pursue what you know you deserve in life. Take action now and begin to set some uncommon goals that you want to be remembered for forever. Go ahead and write them down in your journal and watch how God will begin to activate things in your life, simply because you took the first step to take action toward something new and rare.

Getting God's Attention

How do you get God's attention? This is a question that has been asked by many people, many times over. Well, I have the answer. If you sincerely desire to get God's attention you can only do so by pleasing Him. God will pay close attention to you then. The only way to please God is to pursue something so uncommon that it requires uncommon faith in order to obtain it. We're not talking about something mediocre or real easy to get, I mean something so extraordinary that everybody will know that it took genuine faith in God in order to receive it.

Why is it that faith is the only thing that brings pleasure to God? Let's face it, God has everything, does whatever He chooses, and is everything all within Himself. There is nothing that God lacks. God needs nothing. But there is one thing that God desires, and that is to live His life through you and I. The only way that He can experience life in us and through us is when we choose to pursue impossible feats by faith. All throughout the Bible there are many incidences where you can find people who lived extraordinary lives by simply believing in an extraordinary God.

But there is one thing that God desires, and that is to live His life through you and I.

I'm not suggesting that any of these people had power aside from God. What I am saying is that these people recognized the power of God in them, so strong, that they knew that with God, they were invincible. One of my favorite Books in the Bible is the book of Hebrews, primarily because it is the book that lists the many uncommon men and woman of faith. We could properly title Hebrews chapter eleven, "Uncommon Achievers." Not all of these people listed there were the most perfect people. No one is perfect. Although all of these people were so different in many ways, they all had one thing in common; they all pursued uncommon avenues to demonstrate their amazing faith in God.

By faith Enoch was taken away so that he did not see death, "and was not found, because God had taken him"; for before he was taken he had this testimony, that he pleased God. But without faith it is impossible to please Him, for he who comes to God must believe that He is, and that He is a rewarder of those who diligently seek Him. —Hebrews 11:5-6

Just look at Enoch's faith, his faith caused something so uncommon to occur. He was able to escape death entirely and go from one level of life to another without having to die in order to do so. Every human has to physically die in order to get to the afterlife; it's our way of transitioning. That did not happen with Enoch. His faith kept him alive beyond natural standards. He went from one level of existence to a higher level, just like that. We can look at Enoch as one of the fathers of the faith because he showed us an early example of what it meant to really please God.

Every human has to physically die in order to get to the afterlife; it's our way of transitioning.

There were several people who stood out in this uncommon list of faith-full people. It would take too long to name every one of them. However there are a couple of people who just stand out in my mind as people who pursued an uncommon pursuit against all odds. Rahab is one of the lesser-mentioned characters in the Bible yet her story is quite uncommon. First, Rahab was actually called Rahab the harlot. She was a woman who ran a house that took care of the carnal desires of itinerating professionals traveling through her city.

The religious people would immediately look at her sins, her faults, and shortcomings and reason that God could never use her, because of her awful reputation.

Now I know that for all the religious folks it may be kind of hard to grasp just why God would choose her to be listed amongst such great faith figures, such as Father Abraham. The religious people would immediately look at her sins, her faults, and shortcomings and reason that God could never use her, because of her awful reputation. Unfortunately, that's the way so many people view things, especially Christians. Many people believe that God rewards us according to our sins or our righteousness. Actually, God doesn't reward us for either. God only responds to our faith.

> *By faith the harlot Rahab did not perish with those who did not believe, when she had received the spies with peace. —Hebrews 11:31*

Rahab pursued the uncommon path of believing that God would actually reward her with the blessing of protection and safety for her family if she would dare to hide the spies from the local authorities. How many Christians do you know that would blaze this uncommon path of faith? How many people do you know who would actually deter armed soldiers, believing in a promise without actual proof of that promise? Very few people would pursue such a path. Only the strong in faith would actually follow this route.

God only responds to our faith.

Just think though, Rahab wasn't the kind of woman who had a great reputation, and to most readers it would be far easier to believe in a woman whose name and actions were far more virtuous than hers. Why would anybody trust a prostitute? There's an old saying in the streets that goes, "Never trust the love of a prostitute." This kind of goes without saying, as their job is to make you believe that something that isn't real is actually real. So why would this prostitute suddenly have a change of heart, and want to participate in the practice of covering God's men? Deep within she made a decision to pursue an uncommon path.

Throughout the course of life, you and others will come face-to-face with the opportunity to take a very different path, a faith path that people in your circle may not necessarily believe that you will take. It doesn't matter what people believe about you, what's most important is what you believe about yourself and what God says about you. This woman believed what God's servants promised her. She took them at their word, that's all. And that act alone was not only courageous but most uncommon. Here is a lesson to learn: Don't sabotage your future success because of your past mistakes.

It takes an uncommon person to look
past their failures and shortcomings
and still believe that they are worth
being blessed.

It takes an uncommon person to look past their failures and
shortcomings and still believe that they are worth being
blessed. Are you ready to receive all that God has promised
you? If you are you must be able to look beyond your past
reputation, your past mistakes and failures, and believe that
God's promise for you is far greater than any slip-up you
made. Another person who pursued an uncommon path is
Abraham. As I said earlier, Abraham is connected with the
world's three most well-known religions. He is known as a
Father of the faith movement, because he, too, chose to pursue an uncommon path. Hebrews 11:17-19 gives us insight
into the path that he chose.

> *By faith Abraham, when he was tested, offered up*
> *Isaac, and he who had received the promises*
> *offered up his only begotten son, of whom it was*

*said, "In Isaac your seed shall be called," conclud-
ing that God was able to raise him up, even from
the dead, from which he also received him in a
figurative sense.—Hebrews 11:17-19*

Abraham chose to pursue the lonely path of believing God to do the impossible. God asked him to sacrifice his only begotten son, a type and shadow of Christ, on the altar. Quite honestly, this path would be a difficult one for me to travel, as I can understand first hand how much love a father has for his children. I have two sons whom I love dearly. They both know it. There is nothing that I wouldn't do for them. It would be hard for me to understand at first why God would challenge me with the test of slaying my own sons.

Even if there were a greater promise on the other side, it is still difficult to follow through on this process, not knowing for sure what's going to come out of it. That's why Abraham is dubbed as the Father of faith, because he leads us in the action of taking necessary steps to prove to God that you really trust him. At times your faith will be challenged. You will be required to pursue not only an uncommon path, but also one that is quite unfamiliar. I have come to realize that God really desires for you to just do something—take action.

Your actions toward obedience and believing his Word initiates God's hand in your life. That's what my whole life's teaching boils down to taking action. In life everybody is different, and everybody has different paths to take. But one thing that I know is that everybody is required to do something, to take action. The reason why all of the people listed in Hebrews 11 made it there is because they actually took action.

They did something even if they were uncertain along the way. In your pursuit of following God's higher purpose for your life, what action(s) can you take right now that will activate the process of your pursuit. Rahab's action was simply hiding the spies underneath some flax on top of the roof of her house. Abraham's action was to take his only son and began a procession up to the altar. Your action will be different, but your pursuit will never begin until you do something!

Humanly Impossible

> *"The things which are impossible with men are possible with God." —Matthew 19:26*

Throughout my life and ministry I have done my best to try to encourage people to believe God to do the impossible. The things that people find hard to believe that you can do are the things that God will empower you to do. I've discovered that the blessings of the Lord are not reserved for the rich and famous, but rather those who are rich in faith. Those who believe that God can will actually experience God's favor on an entirely new level. My prayer is that we can actually get back to the time when we trusted God to do the impossible.

Even in a challenging economy, you have to believe that God can and will cause you to be totally prosperous, having all your needs met. It doesn't matter whose getting laid off, or what companies are going out of business. Even in the time of famine God can cause the most unexpected person to increase more and more. What I want you to do is become more open to pursuing the impossible, or should I say what others call impossible. We know that with God all things are possible. Don't label yourself and limit yourself in this hour by wondering if someone has already done what God is calling you to do.

We know that with God all things are possible.

It really doesn't matter who has or hasn't done it before. Perhaps God is calling you to be the first one. Barack Obama became the first African-American president. Neil Armstrong was the first astronaut to travel to the moon. Sir Roger Bannister was a 25 year old medical student at Oxford University who decided to run a 4 minute mile, something that had never been done before. It doesn't matter whether anyone has done it before or not. What matters most is your willingness to pursue this uncommon path and believe that God will use you as a vessel to do what is believed to be humanly impossible.

What matters most is your willingness to pursue this uncommon path and believe that God will use you as a vessel to do what is believed to be humanly impossible.

And I will bless her and also give you a son by her; then I will bless her, and she shall be a mother of nations; kings of peoples shall be from her." Then Abraham fell on his face and laughed, and said in his heart, "Shall a child be born to a man who is

one hundred years old? And shall Sarah, who is
ninety years old, bear a child?" And Abraham said
to God, "Oh, that Ishmael might live before You!"
—Genesis 17:16-18

Consider how ridiculous Sarah must have looked, pregnant
at 90 years old. Her husband's uncommon faith believed
that a promise would come to pass, way past childbearing
years. To my knowledge, there hasn't been anyone since
Sarah who has given birth at 90. I'm certainly not recom-
mending that you go out and try this if you are 90 years old,
but I do believe that it is possible. When God's spirit comes
upon you, it causes you to do and become more than what
is humanly conceivable.

Then it came to pass the seventh time, that he said,
"There is a cloud, as small as a man's hand, rising
out of the sea!" So he said, "Go up, say to Ahab,
'Prepare your chariot, and go down before the rain
stops you.'" Now it happened in the meantime that
the sky became black with clouds and wind, and
there was a heavy rain. So Ahab rode away and
went to Jezreel. Then the hand of the LORD came
upon Elijah; and he girded up his loins and ran
ahead of Ahab to the entrance of Jezreel.
—1 Kings 18:44-46

I know that we have tremendous athletes today. But I don't know of many who can outrun a horse. Here in 1 Kings, the prophet outran the king's chariots after the spirit of the Lord came upon him. This is humanly impossible, but it happened because an ordinary man believed God. Our earth is groaning for the sons and daughters of God to rise up to their rightful places and become the representation of His Kingdom. God is waiting for somebody to be willing to do the humanly impossible. In a society where everybody is afraid, uneasy, and believing that things are going to get worse, God needs you to become just the opposite of their false beliefs. Pursue the impossible, what's never been done before, and let's create a new list of God pleasers, pursuing uncommon paths.

4

Uncommon Words

"If the word has the potency to revive and make us free, it has also the power to blind, imprison, and destroy." —Ralph Ellison

Words have the ability to create life's situations. It doesn't matter whether those situations are good or bad, your words continue to create your reality. If there is anything that I sincerely believe it is that you must understand how to harness the power of your words and use that power to produce uncommon results in this world. Everything that you see and experience in life started first with a word. All creation began with words. In the beginning God created the heavens and the earth, "And then God said..." Before anything is created it must first be spoken. God showed us this pattern from the beginning.

So if everything that exists began with words, then you must begin to look at the words you are speaking to evaluate what kind of return you are receiving, and, of course, what you are creating. What are you saying and what is coming into your life as a result of what you are saying? There are literally hundreds of thousands of words in the English language. There are millions more words in languages all around the world, but there are some words that are common. When I say common, I don't mean that the words are meaningless or that the words do not have any power at all.

It's just that some words have become so commonly used that they just don't carry the same kind of authority that uncommon words carry. People have used them and over-used them so that they've kind of lost their effectiveness. People don't take them as seriously. For example, when a person asks you "How are you doing?" most people respond by saying "I'm doing good." Both the question and the answer are usually common. The truth is, most people aren't really all that concerned about how you are really doing. It's just become a common way to greet people.

Imagine if someone actually began to tell you exactly how he or she were feeling, and took up a couple of hours in doing so. You may probably feel as if they were wasting your time. You wouldn't be expecting a real honest answer, since most people answer that question in a common way. When you choose to speak words that are only common you will only receive common results. But when you dare to speak words that are uncommon then you automatically upgrade yourself to a higher level. That is the level of life that I am convinced that God wants you to live on.

When you choose to speak words that are only common you will only receive common results.

Going to a higher level doesn't always come through education, although education is wonderful. Going to that next level in life can be easily connected to your ability and willingness to begin speaking new words, words that are not the expected norm. Faith words are what elevate you to your higher purpose in God. In order to see great things in your life begin to happen, you have to start speaking it. Regardless of the circumstances or whatever you may be going through, you have to speak bold uncommon words against the odds. You have to say what you expect rather than what you are experiencing. You have to speak the words that you want to experience.

You have to speak the words that you want to experience.

In order to continually speak words that are uncommon and get results that are uncommon, you have to shed yourself of the image that people had of you before. One of the things that people, especially family and friends, will do is place you in a box. They will limit you by what they believe you are capable of doing based on what you have done before. That is why I am here to teach you how to live above the limitations of people. Your past is not your future unless you continue to say the same things that you have always said, then you will get what you have always had.

Right now just free yourself from any past limitations by say-ing these uncommon words, "I AM NOT MY PAST." Go ahead and say it now! If you want to see different things happening in your life, you will have to begin to change your words to match the things that you want to see. You'll have to learn to start using uncommon words! With perfecting any skill in life, this will take focus and practice. Society has somewhat accepted speaking negative words as being common. And that is probably why there is so much confusion because someone has to be strong enough to speak the positive uncommon words in the midst of negative situations.

God Says You Can

If you have always spoken common words in life, one of the quickest ways to start speaking uncommon words is to begin to believe God's Word concerning you. Whatever God says you are, just accept it as truth, whether it looks like it or not. When you become committed in this area, you will begin to only use words that are consistent with how God feels about you. How does God feel about you? How does He view you in terms of your ability to do great things?

What does God think about your future? Well, God looks at you and says, "You can!" In His eyes there is nothing that you cannot do. God says you can! The way I see it is if God says you can, then how can you argue with God? He believes that your future is promising. Knowing this, you have to latch on to God's mindset and begin believing and saying the same things about yourself that He says.

> *For I know the thoughts that I think toward you,*
> *says the LORD, thoughts of peace and not of evil, to*
> *give you a future and a hope. —Jeremiah 29:11*

We have become so programmed by the negativity of the world that we have embraced what the world believes more than what God believes about us. God never looks at your past and then places limits on you based on that. He does just the opposite. He looks at your past and then decides to use you as an example of how somebody that was ordinary could be used in a marvelous way. But you must get in agreement with God and His plan for your life. It's rather interesting that the God of the universe sees you in a totally different light than other people see you.

In fact, God thinks that it is rather strange when you allow anyone to impede your progress when he has placed so much potential on the inside of you. So if you are going to come into divine order with God you must begin to say what God says. Let me warn you that when you begin speaking like God, you will not be the most popular guy on the block, but God will favor you. You have to make a decision on whether you choose the people's approval or God's favor. For the most part, I have never really looked for anyone's approval.

From the early days of ministry I knew that if I was going to leave a lasting impact on the city of Atlanta that I would have to focus on what I knew I could do. Now, I didn't say that I knew how I would do it. The "how" is not my business. And God never tells me how He does what He does. It really doesn't matter. I would just begin to speak things like we are going on television, and didn't even have a studio. I would say we are going to build a great church for God, yet we were in a storefront.

So you have to recognize that your words have the power to lift you or crush you.

My words didn't make sense in the natural, but in the spiritual realm they were quite clear. I was committed to saying what God was saying. So I took some words totally out of my speech. Never say "I can't." I'll never say that I can't do this or that. When you say "I can't," those very words are actually insulting to God. God says that you can. He is the one who actually performs the work that you are setting out to do, not you. Of your own strength and power, you can't build the multi-million dollar business. You can't build the 10,000-seat dome.

You can't grow the church to thousands. You can't save lives. But the God in you can. So you have to recognize that your words have the power to lift you or crush you. Think about it this way, your words are a self-fulfilling prophecy about what is going to happen in your life. It is a prophecy about what you can and cannot do. So whatever you say, God gives you strength to pursue it. If you say I can't do it. Then God says, "Okay you can't." If you say that you can, then God says, "I agree."

Your words have to be in alignment with God's to produce good things. Because whatever you say you ultimately bring to pass. That is the power of your words. God only uses you as the vessel to perform the work. Your job is to know that He can do anything, and then just become humble enough to accept that truth that you are the chosen one that He wants to do it through.

> *I can do all things through Christ who strengthens me. —Philippians 4:13*

There are right and wrong confessions. All of your confessions ought to agree with God's. God's Word is a continual word, which means that He is always speaking and that His Word has the same power today as it always has. So the goal here is to get you to learn how to agree with God. Wrong confessions are any words that go against God's Word. For example, people in this world will always be challenged by sickness. However, each challenge presents an opportunity to confess the truth of God. So sickness may come against you, but God says, "You are healed!" So it then becomes your obligation to say exactly what God says. "I am healed."

You may have experienced financial difficulty or may be experiencing it right now. The wrong confession is, "I am broke." You will only get more of what you say by confessing that wrong confession. God says He has given you the power to get wealth. So you have to say what God says about your wealth. That is the uncommon road that leads to treasures.

Just One Word

Words are the building blocks for life. That is why the Bible and books that urge people to use positive words are so important. When you begin to speak positive words over your life and the lives of others, amazing things begin to happen. But it's not how many words you say, it's the faith behind the word you speak. Just one word can change everything. I've never been the kind of person who likes to just say a whole lot of words just to say them. When you say words they ought to have purpose.

The very foundation of my ministry and life's mission is that I've always been really concerned with ACTION, and what provokes people to take action in life. Action is not something that is produced by hype or by saying many words. Saying just one word often produces action. Ted Turner, the brainchild behind CNN built a 24-hour news network. The people didn't think it could be done. But he said, "We can do it!" He didn't need to say many words, just a few. And today we see the manifestation of the words he spoke.

When you begin to speak positive words over your life and the lives of others, amazing things begin to happen.

We have witnessed the first African-American president of the United States of America rise from being relatively unknown in national circles to becoming the most popular person in the world. How did he do it? President Barack Obama understood the power of words, and how words can produce amazing results. Imagine that this man won an entire election by campaigning using one word—Change. Talk about the simplicity of words. How could one very simple word make such a difference? Obama realized that our nation was in need of some pretty major changes, and he also understood that the young people in our country were dissatisfied with how things used to be done.

If getting things accomplished in America meant that our government would have to make some adjustments, why not start by getting an African-American elected? The word change became uncommon because of the person behind the word, as well as the faith behind it. Obama could have allowed so many things to discourage him. He wasn't from a political dynasty. He didn't have any experience being in the White House. His seat in the senate was short lived. Despite all of those things, he knew how to use the power of uncommon words. Instead of saying the same old things that everybody else said, he decided to say one word and stick with it until he saw what he was saying—CHANGE.

Just use the one word that works and stick with it until you see change.

Why was this word so uncommon? It was because there were so many people in America that didn't want change, and wanted everything to be the way it always has been. The point is that you really don't have to be the most skillful person with words. Just use the one word that works and stick with it until you see change. There is a scripture in the Bible that displays the power of uncommon words in action.

> *Now when Jesus had entered Capernaum, a centurion came to Him, pleading with Him, saying, "Lord, my servant is lying at home paralyzed, dreadfully tormented." And Jesus said to him, "I will come and heal him." The centurion answered and said, "Lord, I am not worthy that You should come under my roof. But only speak a word, and my servant will be healed. For I also am a man under authority, having soldiers under me. And I say to this one, 'Go,' and he goes; and to another, 'Come,' and he comes; and to my servant, 'Do this,' and he does it." When Jesus heard it, He marveled, and said to those who followed, "Assuredly, I say to you, I have not found such great faith, not even in Israel! And I say to you that many will come from east and west, and sit down with Abraham, Isaac, and Jacob in the kingdom of heaven. But the sons of the kingdom will be cast out into outer darkness. There will be weeping and gnashing of teeth." Then*

Jesus said to the centurion, "Go your way; and as
you have believed, so let it be done for you." And his
servant was healed that same hour.
—*Matthew 8:5-13*

Here we see a centurion who was a commander in the Roman army over one hundred men, which is where we get the word century and centurion. His servant was sick and paralyzed. After telling Jesus about his servant's condition, Jesus agreed to heal the man. The centurion did not feel that he was worthy to have someone as high as Jesus in his house. So he told Jesus all you have to do is speak a word, and my servant will be healed.

The centurion then stated to explain to Jesus how he understood the power and authority of uncommon words. He would tell his soldiers to come and others to go and they would obey his word. So based on that He knew that Jesus' Word would be just as powerful. But check this out, the centurion never asked Jesus to say many words but rather a word, or just one word, and my servant will be healed. That's amazing. It doesn't always have to be many words to get the job done in life; just the right one.

What Are You Creating?

What are you creating with the power of your words? I believe that in this day, there are so many great things just waiting to be accomplished through ordinary people who aren't afraid to just open their mouth and say it. Perhaps you might need to do some research on what has not been done before, and begin to say what you want to see. Every minute of each day you are creating something with each word that you speak. You are building or destroying, planting or uprooting. Nobody is ever in a neutral state; there is no such thing.

With your words you can build up the lives of people all around you.

With your words you can build up the lives of people all around you. From the time my boys were small, I have always made it a priority to speak positive words over them. I understand the power of uncommon words and how it literally shapes our lives, so I am careful to only speak words that will add to, instead of take away from. Think about ways that you can begin to use your words, uncommon words, to build the lives of others, to establish great organizations, to build profitable businesses, great relationships, and better spiritual lives.

Throughout the scriptures Jesus showed the power of His Words. He looked at a fig tree one day and saw that it wasn't producing fruit, and he said, "curse," and immediately the tree was cursed. One day Peter, one of Jesus' disciples tried to walk to Jesus on water, afraid that he might sink, Jesus said one word, COME and Peter was able to do the impossible. Begin to practice using words that will produce a harvest. For whatever you say you shall receive.

5

The Principle of the Uncommon Seed

It is every man's obligation to put back into the world at least the equivalent of what he takes out of it. —Albert Einstein

In this hour, there is nothing more needed than a strong understanding of the principle of the seed. Before we can get to the uncommon seed, we have to first establish the major importance of the seed itself. From the beginning of time, the enemy has done everything possible to attack the one thing that produces everything, and that is the seed. He knows that if he can convince you to do everything with your seed other than sow it into fertile soil that you will never fulfill your God given potential in life. There are so many people who are somewhat afraid to deal with this topic.

God has called me to deal with this so that the Body of Christ will be of free lack and want. It's quite amazing that this principle of the seed is understood and practiced in so many arenas without any controversy except in the church. The church is attacked more than any other institution whenever she decides to deal with this principle. The principle is perhaps one of the most basic principles known to humankind. And, this principle is as old as the earth. It basically goes like this: plant a seed then reap the harvest.

Every farmer understands this simple concept. He prepares the soil for seeding, plants the seeds, continues to water the seeds, and waits for the seed to grow. This is the cycle of life.

Another way of stating this truth is 'whatever a man soweth that he shall also reap.' Every farmer understands this simple concept. He prepares the soil for seeding, plants the seeds, continues to water the seeds, and waits for the seeds to grow. This is the cycle of life. It is understood in all walks of life. It is the principle of giving and receiving. Of all the topics that have been fought against, I can't think of any in the church that has gained more criticism than in the area of giving and receiving.

Even though there are so many people who oppose this principle, especially as it relates to the church, I find that as I travel around the country most requests are for prayer in the area of personal finances. This seems odd that so many people desire to be financially free, yet at the same time, many choose to deny the spiritual process that will bring it about. The enemy will always attack ministry in this area, because he knows that if people embrace this understanding the church will advance rapidly, as the harvest will be won, trained and then sent out to reproduce themselves.

The enemy cannot stop God's progress,
because he is still subordinate to God.

So if the enemy can convince you to not sow the seed into the church then he knows that he can delay the progress of the church, and also delay your blessing. The enemy cannot stop God's progress, because he is still subordinate to God. But he can slow things down. And when that happens we feel the effects of how long and drawn out the process of receiving seems to be. You can't receive what you haven't given. Until you release something on earth, nothing will be released from the heavens. So this is about getting you to understand why it is so important to sow seeds.

Why is it that so many people, even in the church, are challenged in the area of their finances? Well, the main reason people experience these kinds of challenges is because money represents life. You give your life, your hours of work and service in exchange for money. You exchange your life for something of equivalent value. So when you don't have money, in many ways your life has been diminished, as you are limited in the choices that you can experience and enjoy. It is somewhat understandable for a person who is connected to God to have concerns about money.

Until you release something on earth, nothing will be released from the heavens.

After all, we live in a time of tremendous financial unsteadiness. The national debt is still at an all time high. My children and their children won't be able to pay off the debts. It appears that we have entered into a global recession, one that financial experts suggest we may not fully recover from for at least a decade. In my city of Atlanta, unemployment is on the rise. There are people who are losing their homes, and yes, the soup kitchens don't have enough food to meet the demands of the many people who seek their assistance.

I agree that there is a world need that must be satisfied, but I also believe that the church is obligated to be a solution to all of those problems.

So from a natural mindset, it wouldn't be right to actually give money away when times seem so hard. I've heard people justify not giving to the church with excuses such as, "People in Africa are so poor that they don't have anything to eat. We should give to them instead of supporting the church in America." The strange thing is that the people who argue this point do not often give anything to the people in Africa or any other mission field for that matter. I agree that there is a world need that must be satisfied, but I also believe that the church is obligated to be a solution to all of those problems.

The only way we can be a solution is for the storehouse in the local church to remain full, so that it can continue to gift to every good work. Looking at the condition of the world, why then would we continue to ask you to give? God's principles are eternal, and unconditional. This means that we are obligated to continually ask to establish the ground on which blessings are birthed for you. No matter how depleted our global economy may become, we have a higher hope in Christ, who teaches all of humanity to follow His perfect example.

> *For God so loved the world that He gave His only begotten Son, that whoever believes in Him should not perish but have everlasting life.* —John 3:16

This verse, John 3:16, is perhaps the most widely read and definitely the most well-known verse in the entire Bible. It is the foundation for salvation. But it also holds the secret to having an abundant life. Here, Jesus is being offered as the ultimate seed, a sacrificial seed. Once this seed is planted according to the text, everlasting life kicks in. This is interesting! This same principle of the seed applies in your life also. When you plant the seed you initiate the wheels to moving you toward perpetual life, one that continuously regenerates itself.

So it is my mandate and the mandate of all preachers of righteousness to tell everyone the truth concerning God's Word. So your giving is not predicated on whether or not the economy is good. It is based on whether or not there is poverty in the land. There will always be poverty and people who are poor in the earth. Our giving is first an obedient response to God's Word. Secondly, it is an act of faith. I like that. Giving is an action that sets off supply in your life and the life of others. Finally, it is the response of people who live in God's economy, not a failing global financial system.

Our giving is first an obedient response to God's Word. Secondly, it is an act of faith.

When you understand the principle of the seed and activate it, you will discover that God has never needed world circumstances to be favorable before He blessed you. The world could be in the greatest recession of all time, yet you will still live the blessed life when you take action and release the seed. This is an eternal principle that never changes no matter how hard things may appear to be. You sow the seed; you will reap the harvest!

Like gravity forces weighted objects downward, your seed forces heavens storehouse to open and begin to pour out. It's strange to understand how God does it, but that is not your problem. He just does. The pilot doesn't necessarily know exactly how the engine on a plane works, yet he or she continues to navigate the plane, and the passengers feel secure in the hands of the pilot. Just know that by releasing the seed, the only possibility for you is increase, because the blessing of the Lord only multiplies.

> *No one has ever become poor by giving.*
> *—Anne Frank*

She Gave Her Life

> *And He looked up and saw the rich putting their gifts into the treasury, and He saw also a certain poor widow putting in two mites. So He said, "Truly I say to you that this poor widow has put in more than all; for all these out of their abundance have put in offerings for God, but she out of her poverty put in all the livelihood that she had."*
> *—Luke 21:1-3*

This passage tells the remarkable story of a lady who sowed an uncommon seed. The Bible says that she was a widow. In that time, when a woman's husband died, leaving her widowed, she was left to bear the responsibility of paying all of her husband's debts as well as current ongoing expenses such as food and clothing. So for the most part, most women in this position either died from starvation shortly after the husband died, or they would be subjected to prostitution to take care of themselves. If they had a male child, then he would become the sole provider for his mother and the executor of his father's estate.

...this lady recognized that she needed to sow a seed in order to free herself from her condition.

But in this story we don't see any record of this lady having a son or anyone willing to help her in her state. Having no one to help her, this lady recognized that she needed to sow a seed in order to free herself from her condition. There were rich people giving their offering, but this woman gave two mites and put it in the offering. Two mites were only worth $1/64^{th}$ of a days wage. To the rich her offering was pretty meaningless, but to Jesus her offering was the greatest, as he commented that she had given *all* out of her poverty.

What was uncommon was the fact that she was a common person who had nothing else to put her hands on. She dared to put all that she had into the hands of Jesus. The average person can easily relate to this story about an uncommon seed. It doesn't even have to be about money. You can look at this from the fact that the average person may not have a whole lot of skill. You may not have a Harvard or Yale education. You may not have the best job, or, for that matter, a job at all. You may not live in the best area.

What was uncommon was the fact
that she was a common person who
had nothing else to put her hands on.

The principle here is that she gave all that she had in her hands. She gave all that represented her entire life, and that was totally uncommon. The average person gives what is comfortable for them to give. They give and still have plenty left over. The rich who were giving were giving out of their abundance. That's quite common. It's easy to give a $100.00 or even $1000.00 if you have hundreds of thousands of dollars.

It becomes uncommon when you have hundreds of thousands and you decide to give it all. Whatever the value the widow's mites were, she decided to forfeit what benefit it could be to her and give it. How uncommon to not consider yourself but rather the treasury which supports the needs of others. It is uncommon to give to others need when your need is just as pressing. What a selfless life! She was concerned that the ministry had enough to continue its cause even if it meant that she would be at a disadvantage.

He Gave His Lunch

Now the Passover, a feast of the Jews, was near. Then Jesus lifted up His eyes, and seeing a great multitude coming toward Him, He said to Philip, "Where shall we buy bread, that these may eat?" But this He said to test him, for He Himself knew what He would do. Philip answered Him, "Two hundred denarii worth of bread is not sufficient for them, that every one of them may have a little." One of His disciples, Andrew, Simon Peter's brother, said to Him, "There is a lad here who has five barley loaves and two small fish, but what are they among so many?" Then Jesus said, "Make the people sit down." Now there was much grass in the place. So the men sat down, in number about five thousand. And Jesus took the loaves, and when He

had given thanks He distributed them to the disci-
ples, and the disciples to those sitting down; and
likewise of the fish, as much as they wanted.
—John 6:4-11

Another example of an uncommon seed is in this story. Jesus needed to feed the multitudes and asked his disciple Philip where could they buy bread. Here Jesus is testing his disciple because he knew that there was no place in that region that sold enough bread to feed 5,000 people. Philip gave a common response letting Jesus know that they only had two hundred denarii worth of bread, not enough to feed everyone. Phillip could have taken action and given what he had to Jesus, but instead he did nothing, One of Jesus' "take action" disciples, Peter, noticed that a little boy had a lunch with five loaves and two small fish.

Peter realized immediately that Jesus always maximized uncommon situations. This was the kind of thing Jesus specialized in doing. The little boy offered Jesus his lunch, what little he had in his hand, and Jesus fed 5,000. There were more than 20,000 people including the women and the children. And all of them were fed. In fact, they all ate as much as they wanted. Going to the store and buying groceries would have been common. It would have been the expected norm.

Often we try to do what we are accustomed to doing because it is familiar to us. But God continually prompts us and pushes us out of the place of familiarity into the place of uncertainty to get us to experience a blessing that we've never tasted before. This young boy gave Jesus an unusual seed, and he was able to be a participator in an unusual harvest. The principle of the seed always produces a harvest.

God Will Use Whatever Is In Your Hand

> *So the LORD said to him, "What is that in your hand?" He said, "A rod." —Exodus 4:2*

My whole reason for writing this book is to get you to understand how to walk and operate in the uncommon realm. More than that I want you to take some kind of action to begin the process of allowing God to do great things in your life. Remember real faith is about action, it's about doing something. Real uncommon faith takes all excuses away. You aren't required to do things in a common way; therefore, you can't use that excuse. God expects you to do the uncommon. He expects you to live outside of the norm. When it comes to giving you need to start recognizing creative ways to give.

Perhaps your job is too common of a way for you to offer an uncommon seed to the Lord. Don't focus on your job. Don't focus on anything that has become common for you. Focus on what is uncommon and most unusual and it is that thing, that offering, that God will anoint to become far more than it was when it was given. God is in the business of expansion, and he will cause your uncommon seed to grow and grow. Your resolve needs to be, "I will give whatever is in my hand."

Very often in life you may believe that whatever is in your hand is not enough. Moses, the lawgiver and deliverer, once had this same dilemma. He didn't realize that what he had was more than enough for God to work with. When God asked him to deliver the children of Israel from Pharaoh's bondage, he immediately began to make excuses about why he couldn't do what God asked him to do. Often we see ourselves as insignificant and not having enough to get the job done. God will never ask you to do anything that He has not already equipped you to do.

Your resolve needs to be, "I will give whatever is in my hand."

At the very moment God asks anything of you, whether you realize it or not, the provision is already there. Sometimes we look for the common seed, the common help, and the common resources to show up, because we are too common minded. Moses didn't even recognize that everything he needed to deliver God's people was already in his hand. The rod with all of its power was the uncommon seed needed to deliver a people. He didn't know it at first; Moses had to become aware of his seed.

God's not concerned about your seed fitting in. In fact, God is much more concerned about your seed standing out!

What's in your hand? What talents and gifts do you have to offer as a seed? What can you give that will show an exchange of your life? Whatever that is, give it. You can spend a lifetime waiting to get the right seed, or to give what you believe would be more customary. God's not concerned about your seed fitting in. In fact, God is much more concerned about your seed standing out! A multi-millionaire will have to do more than a poor widow woman to cross over into the uncommon seed zone.

They can't give what is considered standard. Your faith sets the standards. Your ability to stretch beyond the present limitations gets God's attention. Make a quality decision and a strong commitment that from this moment on you will never make an excuse about your seed. You should never say "I don't have it," or "I don't have enough." Those details are unimportant. What matters most is that you know that God will use whatever you have in your hands.

6

Seeing What No One Else Sees:
The Uncommon Vision

"Vision without action is a dream. Action without vision is simply passing the time. Action with Vision is making a positive difference."
—*Joel Barker*

When was the last time you made a difference? The answer to that question is key to so many things about you. The person who is committed to making a difference has to have a vision in place in order to do so. And as I'll continually remind you, your vision must be accompanied with corresponding actions. You must take action! You can have a vision to dig a hole in the ground, but until you pick up the shovel and begin digging, nothing is going to happen. So your action actually sets vision in motion. It could be something as simple as making a phone call to a person who is a link to your financial future.

Just talking about calling the person will not do anything to connect you with your vision. You have to actually take action! Vision is everything. It is what keeps the earth moving on its axis. Vision is what keeps hungry people fed, and gives shelter to the needy. Show me anyone who has done something major to touch the lives of people, and I'll show you someone who was totally obsessed with a compelling vision. At the same time, if you show me anyone who was compelled by a vision, then I will show you a person who had to overcome many obstacles in order to get where they wanted to be.

The truth is that your vision in life will cost you.

The truth is that your vision in life will cost you. There is a price to pay. And you must count the cost to make sure that your vision is worth the journey. Why will your vision cost you? It's not because people just want to fight against you. No, not at all. It's because vision is the one thing in life, that for a while, you may be the only one who can actually see it.

People tend to fight against whatever they cannot see or understand. The bigger your vision, the less people will be able to understand it at first. And if they can't understand it, they can't join in.

People of great vision are not average people. However, the average person can also exercise their vision if they so choose. The average person doesn't realize there is more to this than meets the eye. When a person dares to be uncommon they find out how much their vision can do. Vision takes the average person from the average realm and places them in the realm of great people. If having vision is something major, just imagine what it is like to have an uncommon vision. An uncommon vision is a vision that has not been done before.

An uncommon vision is a vision that has not been done before.

It's going into a realm that hasn't yet been explored. It is one thing to follow a pattern that has already been established for you, but it's a totally new thing when you chart brand new territory. At first you may be at odds with people because you are not only doing something different but you're doing it differently than the rest of the people who already tried to do it before. Long before IBM computers discovered Bill Gates, the visionary, they were doing what they did best, leading the computer industry in manufacturing.

I do know that he was compelled by this force, and nothing in the world would stop him from seeing and embracing the real experience in his mind

They just didn't know exactly what kind of visionary Gates was. They hadn't recognized his full potential. He didn't just have a vision. He had an uncommon vision. After leaving IBM, Gates opened up his own company because he had a vision that was much larger than what he saw at IBM. They had a set pattern, but his uncommon vision took him beyond the pattern. He did what no one else was doing and few dare to do today. Talking about vision, I've always been amazed by the fact that he chose to call his new software application Windows ™.

I wonder what window he was actually looking through, and what he might have seen looking through that window. I wonder if he saw that every PC in the world would have to use this application. I wonder if he saw through that window Microsoft becoming the richest company in the United States, making Gates the richest man in the world. Whether or not he knew all that would come of his uncommon vision, I don't know. I do know that he was compelled by this force, and nothing in the world would stop him from seeing and embracing the real experience in his mind.

Seeing What No One Else Can See

For our light affliction, which is but for a moment, is working for us a far more exceeding and eternal weight of glory, while we do not look at the things which are seen, but at the things which are not seen. For the things which are seen are temporary, but the things which are not seen are eternal.
—2 Corinthians 4:17-18

The things which cannot be seen have an eternal value to them. Now, when I say that it cannot be seen, it is obvious that someone is seeing it. The person with the uncommon vision sees what others cannot see. People of uncommon faith are usually people with uncommon vision who don't feel bad when others don't see things the way they do. In fact, they actually get motivated when other people can't see what they see. Michael Jordan, who I believe is the greatest basketball player of all time, talks about this whole idea. Michael is a man with an uncommon vision.

You see, it doesn't always matter what others see in you, but it always matters how you see yourself.

A common vision would have been to win one NBA championship in your career. That would have been really commendable. But the uncommon visionary saw six championship wins in his mind. That's uncommon, and to many it was almost unheard of. Even when Michael was in college, his coach selected four other players to be on the cover of ESPN magazine representing North Carolina State University. The coach didn't choose Michael, because he didn't see in him what Michael saw in himself, the greatest player. You see, it doesn't always matter what others see in you, but it always matters how you see yourself.

Michael was very disappointed by what he thought was his coach's bad call. Jordan thought he should have been on the front cover of that magazine. From that moment, he got motivated to prove to himself, and the entire world why he should have been the one chosen to be on the front cover of ESPN. From that time, all the way to being inducted into the Basketball Hall of Fame, Michael has proven over a thousand times why his coach made the wrong choice. In all actuality, his coach made the right choice. That front cover space was not an adequate honor for the kind of player Michael is.

When God gives you an uncommon vision, you never let what people say or do cause you to go backward.

His rejection set him up for a higher level of greatness. It made him challenge himself on a totally different level. When God gives you an uncommon vision, you never let what people say or do cause you to go backward. When people don't see it, you work even harder to make sure that no one misses the uncommon vision given to you. Your commitment to your vision causes others to see it in time.

Daring To Be Different

Walt Disney, the founder of the theme park that bears his name, and the creator of Mickey Mouse, Minnie Mouse, Donald Duck, Goofy and a host of other Disney characters, saw what no one else saw. I never discredit anybody's vision. I always do my best to encourage people to believe that they can do anything. But I'm not so sure that I would have initially been sold on the idea of a talking Mouse and his friends creating a community that would fascinate the world. It didn't matter whether Walt Disney had my vote or not.

If I had to sum up the mindset of the person with an uncommon vision it would be a person who believes that anything is possible.

He dared to be different, seeing what no one else saw, and waiting for the manifestation of his mind's labor to become a living reality. Many people don't know that Mr. Disney never got to see his theme park before he died. Some consider that such a misfortune. But when those closest to him were told that same thing, they disagreed saying, Walt saw this theme park long before anyone ever came here. I believe that. Walt saw it in his mind. He dared to be different.

Barack Obama dared to be different campaigning on a trail that few African-Americans traveled. I'm sure that those who went before him paved the way for him to be where he is today as he readily admits. But something was different about him. He really believed that he could and would become the President of the United States of America. Many African Americans didn't think it was possible, looking at history and believing that the mindset of Americans hadn't changed. Regardless of those who couldn't see it, he still held this uncommon vision in mind and wouldn't let it go.

To all those who thought that it would never happen, Obama continually reminded, "Anything is Possible." If I had to sum up the mindset of the person with an uncommon vision it would be a person who believes that anything is possible. It doesn't matter if what is being pursued never happened before, the uncommon visionary will hold that belief so strongly inside that everything around them begins to fade, as the promise of their vision begins to grow and grow, consuming all of their mental energy. The person with uncommon vision sees nothing other than their vision coming to fruition. Everything else is cloudy, while the vision is clear.

Being the Best at Being You

I will praise You, for I am fearfully and wonderful-
ly made; Marvelous are Your works, And that my
soul knows very well.
—Psalm 139:14

When you have an uncommon vision it comes not only with its struggles, it also comes with it benefits. The struggle is basically getting over the fact that people at first won't recognize your vision as being real. The struggle is just dealing with being misunderstood. So you've got to get over not being recognized. When I first started pastoring in Atlanta, I didn't have a group of pastors rallying around me to support me. In fact, I really can't think of anyone that was there to help me. They did what they were doing, and didn't really extend a helping hand to me. I was in a position of being all alone.

The struggle is just dealing with being misunderstood.

Looking back, that was the best position for me to ever have been in. Having no one to recognize my vision made me rely totally on God. Sometimes when you have an overabundance of support, you tend to rely more on the support than you do on God. Once that support leaves then everything that you have built starts going down. So you've got to face it, that sometimes you may not have the support of your peers, and at times you may not be understood. Most uncommon visions are not easy to understand at first. They are way out there and seem pretty far-fetched. That's how you know the vision is from God.

Trying to be someone else suffocates your ability to be unique.

The benefit of having an uncommon vision is that you will always be number one at being you. One of the things that I am thankful for is that I have never wanted to be anybody but me. I don't say that just to say it, I really mean it. I hope that you share the same attitude regarding this. Trying to be someone else suffocates your ability to be unique. It kills your uncommonness when you aren't confident in who you are. There are hundreds of thousands of pastors and spiritual leaders all over the world.

Many of them are great communicators and innovative leaders. I am always open to learning from people who have a proven record of being leaders in their area of expertise. However, I have no desire to be them. God made me who I am for a reason and I am more than happy with what He has made me into. The reason that I mention this is because I mentor so many young people all over the United States, and I become troubled when I see them trying so hard to become somebody else.

The truth is, they already have an uncommonness about them that is so unique that if they only focused on their uniqueness it would launch them into worldwide success. They continue to look at the success of others and mimic them. God's desire is that you become satisfied and confident about what He has given you—your own uniqueness. It is out of that uniqueness that your uncommon vision will be revealed. The more you try to be someone else, the less your vision will show forth.

God's desire is that you become satisfied and confident about what He has given you—your own uniqueness.

The more that you try to be who God told you to be, you will get greater clarity about who God wants you to be. Everything that I learn from great leaders I take it, and package it into my desire to help people take action. Using their skills helps me to be better at what I am called to do. That only happens when I am totally confidant in who God has made me to be.

Tapping Into Your Uncommon Vision

When you tap into your uncommon vision you do not have to worry about coming up with a theme or idea. In other words you won't have to create your vision out of thin air. The vision that you have, God has already placed inside of you. The way that you can recognize it is that you are extremely passionate about seeing it come into your reality. People of uncommon faith have the ability to do what no one else is doing. Their faith is not dependent on what other people are doing. They don't need the approval of others. They simply hear the voice of God inside telling them to do something, and they just do it!

What compels us to keep doing extraordinary things in spite of the odds is that uncommon visionaries tend to make whatever our vision is our obsession. We become totally involved in whatever the assignment is that God gives us, no matter what it is. It doesn't matter whether it is building a structure, healing the sick, or stretching out in faith to purchase a jet, the uncommon visionaries simply see it and just do it. I know that this can sound somewhat strange to the average person, but this is the mark of how ordinary people tap into the uncommon vision. Never second-guess what you are seeing. That will only prolong your process. Even if you don't know how the job is going to get done, by simply stepping out and doing something, large or small, toward activating your vision, you will be closer to seeing your vision come to past. You've got to do something! I believe that faith can drive your passion and your passion can drive your faith. What are you passionate about? The answer to that question is the secret to your uncommon vision.

I believe that faith can drive your passion, and your passion can drive your faith.

You ask, "What do you mean by passion?" What is that thing that drives you every moment of the day, that you have to have, have to do, or have to become? That is your passion! You don't have to make up a passion. Your passion is God given. It already exists in you. You simply have to tap into it. Once you do, you will find the center of your life's purpose and begin to find meaning on a totally new level. It's not a secret: your passion is something that cannot be hidden for long. People will know what your passion is!

Your passion is God given. It already exists in you.

Venus and Serena Williams' passion is obviously being the best in the world at the game of tennis. Michael Jordan's passion is the game of basketball. Warren Buffet's passion is investing, something he has been doing faithfully since he was 12 years old. Stevie Wonder is passionate about singing, writing, and performing his music. Bishop T.D. Jakes' passion is preaching and giving hope to the hopeless. Billy Graham's passion is winning souls to Jesus. My highest desire is that I live my life so that I will be known and identified by my passion in life.

I've always been passionate about teaching people how to take action. This is nothing I just made up. It's how God wired me. Every part of me is driven to help as many people as I can learn how to not just talk faith, but to act on their faith. So many people in our world talk a lot about what they want to do, and what they are going to do someday. When I hear talk like this, it disturbs me, because my feeling is that what you are going to do someday, you can do it today!

I am a strong believer that you can always do something right now to take action in the direction that you are moving toward. What can you do today that will cause you to get closer to God's vision for your life? It doesn't have to be a major step. It can be something small. The bottom line is that you should do something. Take action! That's my passion. So everything that I do and that I will become in life will be built around my passion. My "uncommonness" will be birthed from that passion as well.

7

God

In the beginning God . . .

Of course we always save the best for last. God is the One who gives all vision and who is the founder of your faith. The God who gives you uncommon faith is not uncommon at all. Actually we cannot put a label on God. God is just who He is. The Bible says He is alpha and omega, beginning and the end. He is actually more than that, because He started the beginning. To make God uncommon would mean that at some point He was common. And He has never been in either category. That is what makes Him so special.

The first four words in the Bible are, "In the Beginning God." Four represents the number of foundation. And those four words represent the foundation for everything that we will ever need to know concerning our faith—God. God started this whole thing. It is up to Him to keep it going and then finish it. So if we are to embrace life and walk in an uncommon faith, we have to have a healthy respect and knowledge concerning the one who gave it to us in the first place. You see; your desire to do great things didn't originate with you. It was all God.

God gave you the initial thought, and then placed desire in your heart, and then gave you the faith to get the job done. All of the strange and way-out ideas that you have—that once acted upon may change the world—God gave them to you. It's interesting how God puts this big reservoir of His power and blessings out there. Whenever you desire it, He places all on the inside of you. God wants you to become like Him in terms of visions and pursuits. And in order for that to happen He places uncommon visions on the inside of us.

He places uncommon visions on the inside of us.

As we begin to pursue the vision and call within us, it takes us on a journey where with each step we become more like Him, knowing that all things are possible. That is why I am so passionate about the underdog in life. I love to minister to the common man and show them a glimpse of what could be if they would only surrender their life, mind and soul to God. God invites a common people to walk out the destiny that He has set for them. He doesn't look at their past. Unlike mankind, He never holds that against them.

God's original intent is that you be uncommon.

It doesn't matter whether you were addicted to drugs, using crack everyday, pushing the needle, or chose the path of crime and were incarcerated for as long as you can remember; God's original intent is that you be uncommon. And He will orchestrate events in your life in such a way that will cause you to surrender to His plan for your life. I have seen it many times over, how God used a person that society threw away and cast off as a loser, someone that would never be anything in life.

I've seen family members write that person off and just waited for them to die. In amazement I have watched God totally transform them and elevate them to become some of the most respected ministers, leaders, educators, and business people in society. How did this happen? It happened because of God. God has a supernatural ability to transform even the wicked heart. It is God's original intent for humanity to live above limitations placed on them by society, tradition, and even familiar spirits. He wants you to break out of the mold that other people have fashioned you into.

God has a supernatural ability to transform even the wicked heart.

Grab a hold of the fact that you were not intended to be common in the first place! Because you chose the common path, it created a fertile ground for God to be able to show off His mighty power in you. There is a false belief that some people were destined for failure and defeat, and that there was nothing they could have done about it. It was just their fate in life. That just isn't true. People are not destined by God to fail and be defeated in life. First, there is no failure or defeat in God and God cannot impart to a person something that is not within Himself.

God doesn't have defeat to offer because it isn't in Him. He can only give you what He has to offer. Some people have argued that the man on the streets was destined to be an addict. That may be someone's process in life, but that certainly isn't his destiny. There certainly is a difference. If you were destined to be on drugs then why didn't God make all the drugs in the world readily available to you? If it was your destiny wouldn't that be more fulfilling than just a three minute high?

I'm being a bit sarcastic on purpose. I'm just making the point that you are called to live life at the highest level. And on your way to that point, enjoy and learn from your process, but also remember that your final destination is to arrive at the place called uncommon faith. That is God's best for you. That is His ultimate vision for your life.

Miracles, God, and Daily Preparation

"You had better live your best and act your best and think your best today; for today is the sure preparation for tomorrow and all the other tomorrows that follow"
—Harriet Martineau, English essayist and novelist

God does work miracles, but they are just that. They are miracles. I'm a firm believer in miracles and can't argue against them. I have seen them working in my life and definitely in the lives of many people who I have had the privilege of serving in ministry. Miracles are fascinating! That I cannot question. But to live your life everyday in search of a miracle can become counterproductive. It somewhat undermines the whole purpose and teaching of walking by faith and not by sight. Faith is a discipline. It is a practice.

Faith is something that becomes perfected because you have done it so many times that it has become second nature.

Faith is something that becomes perfected because you have done it so many times that it has become second nature. For some people who are strong in faith, not to walk by faith is rather awkward because that is all they know how to do. God intends that we walk in His power on a daily basis, not every time we need a miracle. Michael Jordan didn't just become as great as he is because he woke up one day and just started dribbling a ball and soaring through the air. No, that's not how it happened at all. Michael worked his gift through much discipline and focused practice.

On top of that Jordan ate right, avoided junk food, and went far beyond the required workout every single day. He prepared by practicing long hours, hitting the court even when his teammates had finished. Imagine if Michael went out to play each game, and during halftime he ran out to the middle of the court and started crying out for a miracle. Not only would it be quite embarrassing, it would also be unnecessary. Miracles are a bonus. So if you get one, be thankful, but realize that you can create a miracle in your life as you begin to walk under the daily blessings of the Lord. That is how you position yourself for miracles. The good things in life come to those who are prepared.

The good things in life come to those who are prepared.

This same concept works in the area of spirituality. Some people want to become spiritual giants yet do not put in the time to make it happen. They are not exercising discipline and preparing. They never study the Bible, and they rarely set aside time to pray. How can they ever accomplish great spiritual things if they refuse to do these fundamental things?

Some things only come by fasting and prayer, but it takes discipline to do that. Once you began to make preparation a part of your life in everything that you do, especially in spiritual matters, you will begin to appreciate God's process for making people become great. It doesn't happen overnight, it's a lifetime of commitment and a lifetime of reward.

This year a pilot for U.S. Airways, Chesley Sullenburger, had to make an emergency landing on Flight 1549 after several Canadian geese flew into the engine. These weren't just ordinary birds, but rather large birds with a six-foot wingspan that caused pretty bad damage to the plane. He safely landed the plane in the Hudson River, saving the lives of all 155 passengers and crewmembers that were onboard. When asked how he did it, Sullenburger said, "I trained my entire life for this one moment."

Wow, what a powerful statement. This man prepared his entire life for just one moment. He put in a lifetime of preparation for one thing. John the Baptist understood this principle as he prepared his entire life to preach one simple message—repent. Jesus prepared for one moment. His preparation caused him to be able to endure the cross, the pain, and the suffering for a greater cause, seeing humanity come to God. The Bible teaches this principle.

Jesus prepared for one moment.

This doesn't cancel out miracles. There are a lot of people who have diseases and are still alive, because they have a will to live. That is where God intervenes and grants them a miracle. On the same hand, miracles don't cancel out preparation. When I started in the ministry, I prepared. I had no idea that I was going to experience all that I am doing today. I wasn't the most experienced guy at all. I was just starting out.

My thought was then and now, I'm going to put myself in the room where God's blessings are flowing and when they start coming on strong, God won't have to look for me, I'll be right there. My whole approach was I was going to be out there doing what I could do and what I was supposed to do. With that kind of mindset I knew that something good would happen to me, because I was prepared for the blessing to come. Was it all good, back then? No it wasn't.

There were many times that I suffered. However, all things were working together for the good. I never thought that I was greater than Jesus, and He was my ultimate example. Jesus learned from the things he suffered. I, too, learned from the things I suffered. Like weight training, it was painful and it hurt. But after all of the working out my (spiritual) body really does look nice. Greatness never happens overnight, it happens over time, a time of preparation.

Making Me Totally Rely On God

In looking at my personal life and the life of many great leaders, I have noticed a particular pattern that God performs. God strips the support away from us in the beginning and sometimes even as we grow. We sometimes wonder why He does this. So you want to be a businessperson. You thought that your first forty clients were going to come from the church that you've faithfully attended for the past twenty years. Then you discover that the pastor told the church not to do business with you. The reason why he said it is unclear, but it really doesn't matter at this point, your plan failed and now you have to seek out new ideas.

You plan on becoming a major community leader and start playing your hand at politics. Then you find out that your best friend started to trump-up charges against you, bringing up stuff from your past that happened so long ago that you literally forgot all about it. Why do things like this happen? You decide on exposing an evildoing in society that has been perpetuated throughout the past 400 years. When you start speaking against the sins of the fathers, you expect that you would at least have the support of your spiritual sons and daughters, especially since you are the Apostle of Faith.

Instead of getting their support, you find out that you are being criticized and harshly opposed. Your sons and daughters abandon you rather than support your vision. I know how badly this can hurt. The reason why I gave these true-life examples is because God often brings us to this point for one reason, and that is to cause us to become totally reliant on Him all over again. God will flip the script and change all the rules right after you've got them down pat. The ones that you thought would be with you to the end will be the ones that will abruptly abandon you for no legitimate reason.

Help comes to those who pursue after the uncommon vision for that sole purpose, the passion of it.

They may not have a reason, but I surely know why God allows these situations to occur. God wants to continually introduce his ways, his methods, new people, new family, and even new money in your life. Getting too comfortable with the "old way" may cause you to become less pliable in God's hands. Your pursuits should be motivated by one thing—God. Help comes to those who pursue after the uncommon vision for that sole purpose, the passion of it. S. Truett Cathy, the founder of the Chick-fil-A restaurant chains, says of uncommon passion, "If you love your work, you'll never have to work again."

So when I need clarity, strength, and direction, I need not consult anyone other than Him.

You do it for the love of it and the passion of it. You do it because God has charged you with the uncommon faith to accomplish and uncommon vision and no matter what you just can't let it go. Be encouraged, you are in great company. I'm one of those who God touched many years ago, and just can't seem to stop running. The difference between then and now, is that I know well who is the One who fuels this massive vision. So when I need clarity, strength, and direction, I need not consult anyone other than Him.

And the LORD answered me, and said, Write the vision, and make it plain upon tables, that he may run that readeth it. For the vision is yet for an appointed time, but at the end it shall speak, and not lie: though it tarry, wait for it; because it will surely come, it will not tarry. Behold, his soul which is lifted up is not upright in him: but the just shall live by his faith.

—*Habakkuk 2:2-4 (King James Version)*

About the Author

Bishop Wiley Jackson is the Presiding Prelate and Founder of Gospel Tabernacle with four flourishing locations in Atlanta, Fayetteville, Griffin, and Stone Mountain, Georgia. For more than twenty-five years he has passionately led his congregations with his intentional message of "ACTION LIVING." Taking action is Bishop Jackson's personal message, his philosophy of life, and his calling, as he has coached many pastors, business and community leaders, and entrepreneurs into taking the necessary steps to elevate their effectiveness.

Bishop Jackson believes that anyone can improve the quality of his or her life by simply taking action, and he motivates average people to do great things by simply doing something that they've never done before. Bishop Jackson is a graduate of Beulah Heights University in Atlanta, Georgia. He is also the recipient of two honorary Doctorates of Divinity. Bishop Jackson founded the Gospel Tabernacle Churches International (GTCI), a fellowship that empowers pastors to build strong churches with the Word of God as their foundational basis.

Bishop Jackson also serves as the Chaplain to the Apostle of Faith, Frederick K. C. Price of Ever Increasing Faith Ministries in Los Angeles, California. Bishop Jackson is an author of books that teach and inspire people to conquer the past, master their present, and embrace the future. He believes that anyone can prevail over life's obstacles by turning negative experiences in life from excuses into stepping-stones. Bishop Jackson resides in the thriving Atlanta metropolis with his wife Mary, and their sons, Wiley III and Paul Emerson.

For More Information

For information regarding speaking engagements, please send email to writewiley@wileyjackson.org , or written correspondence to Wiley Jackson, P.O. Box 339, Stone Mountain, Georgia 30086